The Lost Churches and Chapels of Kent

Alex Vincent

S.B. Publications

First published in 2005 by S. B. Publications
Tel: 01323 893498
Email: sbpublications@tiscali.co.uk

ISBN 1-85770-302-2

Front cover pictures: Snave, Midley, Court-at-Street, Horne's Place Chapel
Back cover: Dode

Designed and Typeset by EH Graphics (01273) 515527
Printed by Ethos Productions Ltd.

Introduction

Throughout the country there are a vast number of lost churches and chapels either standing in ruins, no visible remains above ground, or redundant. In the case of the former, some may have several walls remaining, only a few stones, just foundations, or could be complete, but roofless. In the case of no visible remains above ground, an earthen mound or earthworks may mark their sites and in some cases only the graveyard remains. Some sites have been built over and a plaque sometimes marks them. In redundant churches, they are either not in use or have only a few services each year.

The loss of churches and chapels can be for several reasons and one is neglect where the parishioners were too poor to repair them. Another is the desertion of the village which it once served. In most lost villages the church still stands today and is in use, serving other nearby settlements, which either lost their church or never possessed one. Some churches came out of use at the Dissolution of the Monastries, and French attacks, war etc are other reasons why they became lost. Some ruined churches were rebuilt, incorporating the remains of the original into the new, such as at Durrington and Aldrington in Sussex.

A number of churches and chapels have been lost to the sea by coastal erosion and the most famous case is at Dunwich in Suffolk. This was once a city, which had a fair number of churches and chapels now lost beneath the waves between the 12th and 20th centuries. The east coast of Britain suffered much coastal erosion over the centuries. Rocks visible at low tides are said to be the remains of a church, but any building would have crumbled away in the sea. In most cases of churches out at sea, there is a legend that the bells can still be heard chiming in the tower at certain times of the year.

Lost churches and chapels come into three categories, which are 1. just its site where there are no visible remains, 2. standing in ruins, and 3. still a complete church, but in use as some other function or derelict. In the case of the latter, only its original use is lost and could well become a place of worship again in the future. Some churches and chapels are only partly lost, where only the chancel for example is in use, but the nave is either in ruins or nothing remaining above ground such as at Lullington in Sussex.

The sites of lost churches and chapels (ruins, no visible remains etc.) are mainly owned by someone such as the National Trust, English Heritage, or in private ownership. Permission must be sought to visit those on private land, but some can be seen from nearby footpaths. Others are just overgrown ruins by a farm, in a field or woodland, but in most cases a footpath passes close by. Some ruins can be dangerous (particularly those which are overgrown) and care must be taken to visit them. If in doubt then it is best not to go into them and only view them from the nearby footpath or road. This also applies to churches lost beneath the waves, where the sea can be a dangerous place, and cliff edges which can be very treacherous, so care must be taken at very low tides and at the top and bottom of cliffs.

This book gives details of the lost churches and chapels in Kent and all photographs were taken by the author. Of places which had more than one church in Medieval times, which are mentioned under the one heading, then the photograph is of the title such as Canterbury All Saints. Where the title does not mention any particular church, like Hastings parish churches, then the accompanying photograph will be mentioned in the text such as "pictured here". This will also apply to where the site of the lost church or chapel is uncertain if there is more than one possible site for it. The lost churches and chapels in this book date from the Medieval period or earlier, unless they were rebuilt in Victorian times, but are now lost.

Acknowledgements

I wish to thank those who have helped with the preparation of this book such as various archaeological societies, libraries, record offices and friends. I also thank those who gave me permission to photograph lost churches and chapels, which are on their land. Special thanks also go to the National Trust and English Heritage for giving me permission to photograph sites owned by them.

Alex Vincent. 2005.

Contents

Blackmanstone

The village of Blackmanstone some three miles north of New Romney, was mentioned in the Domesday Book as "Blachemenestone" and a church was also recorded. This church, like the others on the Romney Marsh, was built by the Lord of the Manor. In 1292 a visitation Roll records "mass wont to be celebrated in the said church of Blackmanstone every day". The church probably consisted of a nave and chancel. It may also have had a tower.

The church probably became lost after the village was deserted in the Middle Ages and was in ruins by the 16th century. Today nothing is visible above ground and stones from the ruins were re-used and incorporated into a farm, an onlooker's hut and also in the repairs of Blackmanstone Bridge. The site of the church (pictured here) is situated in a field to the west of the road some 250 yards north of the bridge. The plough turns up Medieval stones from the church.

Buckland

The village of Buckland some three miles west of Faversham was mentioned in the Domesday Book as "Bocheland", but no church was recorded. The church, which was dedicated to St Nicholas, was built in the Norman period and consisted of a tower, spire, nave and chancel. It has been in ruins since the 18th century. In 1719 the spire was still standing and by the early part of the 18th century the roof had fallen but the north and south walls plus the west end were still standing. Today only the west wall and a small part of the north and south walls of the nave remain in overgrowth near the farm.

Burham

The parish church at Burham in the Medway Valley, dedicated to St Mary, dates from the 12th century and is on the site of an earlier building mentioned in the Domesday Book. It consists of a Perpendicular tower, nave and south porch. There was at one time a north chapel and north and south aisles, and arcades are visible on the north wall of the nave. There is a west window on the tower plus diagonal angle-buttresses.

In the nave are two Norman windows, one on the south wall and the other on the north wall. The latter is blocked. Inside the church is a Norman square bowl font, which has arches on each side and several monuments. The church closed for worship in 1881 when the village moved to higher ground where a new church was built. The old church remains empty, but it was restored from dereliction in 1956.

Burleigh

Burleigh, some one and a half miles west of Charing, once had a manor and Medieval chapel. There is little information about the latter's history of when it was built or when it became disused and left to decay. Burleigh Manor, which stood nearby, was formed of a two-bay hall and was demolished in 1975. It is uncertain if this manor had any connection with the chapel at all or did it serve a settlement which once existed at Burleigh?

The remains of a building in a field north of Burleigh Farm are said to be the remains of the chapel. According to old Ordnance Survey maps this building is marked "Chapel (Rems of)" and is the same building which is referred to as "Chapel ruins at Burleigh Farm" from List of Buildings of Special Architectural or Historic Interest". On the site today the fragmentary remains of the stone chapel stand on a mound.

Canterbury All Saints

In Medieval times Canterbury had a total of 22 parish churches of which 18 were within the walls and four outside. They were All Saints, Holy Cross, St Alphege, St Andrew, St Dunstan, St Edmund Ridingate, St George the Martyr, St Helen, St John, St Margaret, St Martin, St Mary Bredin, St Mary Bredman, St Mary de Castro, St Mary Magdalen, St Mary Northgate, St Mary Queningate, St Michael, St Mildred, St Paul, St Pancras and St Peter.

Only those of St Dunstan, St Martin, St Paul, St Peter and St Mildred are still in use as a place of worship. That of St Martin is the oldest parish church in Britain dating to 560 AD. All the others are lost either in use as another function, stand in ruins, or no visible trace above ground. Besides the parish churches there is a grand cathedral and there were monastic and hospital churches and chapels in Canterbury.

The church dedicated to All Saints dates from the 12th century and consisted of nave, north aisle and south-west tower. The latter was pulled down in 1769 for street widening. The church was rebuilt in 1828 and demolished in 1957. On the site today is a café and the outline of the church is marked by darker bricks in the precinct. A green area with graves to the north was the churchyard.

Canterbury Holy Cross

The church dedicated to Holy Cross was built by Archbishop Sudbury in the latter part of the 14th century. It replaced a chapel which was demolished to make way for the Medieval west gate nearby, which still stands today. Holy Cross consists of a south-west tower, nave, two-bay chancel, south and north aisles and north porch. The trusses on the nave roof consist of four-way struts.

The church was restored in 1860, 1870 and again in 1895. Inside the building is a cup and paten cover of 1585, and several monuments, one of which dates from c. 1600. The church became redundant in 1973 and has been in use as The Guildhall since 1978. Canterbury's original ancient guildhall was demolished in the 1950s. Holy Cross church had a Perpendicular font, which is now in Minster-in-Thanet church.

Canterbury St Alphege

The parish church of St Alphege was probably built by Archbishop Lanfranc in the 11th century on the site of an earlier building of the 7th century. It was rebuilt in the latter part of the 12th and 14th centuries and consists of a tower, pyramid spire, nave and chancel under one roof and north aisle. The church is knapped with flint walls and there are possible Roman foundations on the south wall.

The church has a Perpendicular font with a 17th century cover. There are several monuments inside dating from the 16th to the 19th centuries and one of them is of Robert Casbourne who died in 1523. There is a 14th century two-light window in the north wall of the north aisle, which was once in the south wall of the chancel. The church became redundant in 1982 and is now the Canterbury Environment Centre.

Canterbury St George the Martyr

The parish church dedicated to St George the Martyr dates from the Norman period and was enlarged and extended in 1871, using material from St Mary Magdalen church. A north aisle and new chancel were added. The early Norman building had an apse as excavations had shown. The church consisted of a tower, nave, chancel, south and north aisles. There was Decorated and Perpendicular work in the building.

There were several brasses and monuments in the church and a small churchyard existed to the north-east. The church was destroyed by bomb damage in 1942 leaving it in ruins. Today only the Medieval tower of the church is still standing among modern buildings and shops in the High Street. The tower has a large clock face, which overhangs the street.

Canterbury St Margaret

The church dedicated to St Margaret was built in the 12th century and is situated on the western side of St Margaret's Street. It consists of a tower, nave, chancel, north and south aisles. The eastern end of the chancel was cut off in 1771 to widen the road and the church was restored by Sir G Scott in 1850. The door at the west end of the nave dates from the mid-12th century.

There are several monuments in the church and one is to John Wynter who died in 1470 and Sir George Newman who died in 1627. The church became redundant after bomb damage in 1942, but in 1958 it was opened as a church for the deaf. It finally closed in 1983 and is now in use as the museum for The Canterbury Tales.

Canterbury St Mary Magdalen

The parish church dedicated to St Mary Magdalen dates from the 12th century and stood in Burgate Street. It consisted of a north-west tower, nave, and chancel. The stone tower was built in 1502. The church, except the tower, was demolished in 1871. Some of the materials from the church were used in the building of an aisle to St George the Martyr.

Today only the Perpendicular tower remains on the site and inside it are several 17th century monuments from the old church. One of these is to Henry Saunders who died in 1637 and a tablet to John Whitfield who died in 1691. A Roman Catholic church dedicated to St Thomas was built next to the tower by J G Hall in 1876, which is still in use today.

Canterbury St Mary Northgate

The church of St Mary Northgate dates from the Saxon period and was rebuilt in the 12th century. Its chancel (the original Saxon church) was built over the Roman Northgate hence its dedication. The church consisted of a tower, nave and chancel. It was rebuilt in 1830 and its north wall was built into the Medieval wall of the city. The original chancel became a south aisle at the restoration.

In the north wall are 12th, 14th and 15th century windows and the former is now blocked. At the western end of the church was a late Medieval graveyard. The main 18th century graveyard was on the north side of Broad Street where there are a few graves. The church closed for worship in 1912 and became a parish room. It is now in use as a school gym.

Court-at-Street

The chapel at Court-at-Street some two and a half miles west of Port Lympe, was probably built for the hamlet in the 12th or 13th century. It was called "The chapel of our Lady of Court-at-Street" and consisted of a nave, chancel and a late Perpendicular west doorway. The chapel was made of ragstone and is situated on a slope of a hill just south of the hamlet, overlooking the Romney Marsh.

The chapel fell into ruin sometime in the 16th century, probably after the hamlet was affected by the Black Death. It was inhabited by a hermit after it fell into decay. A nearby pond was used by Pilgrims who came here by the thousand and no doubt worshipped in the chapel. Today parts of the north, west and south walls remain standing and the west doorway is blocked up.

Dode

The Norman church at Dode, south of Luddesdown, was abandoned in the 14th century when the village which it served was deserted by the Black Death. It fell into ruin and was restored in 1905/06. The church was built on a man-made mound. The nearby hill is known as "Holly Hill", which is a corruption of Holy Hill and the narrow lane to the church is called "Wrangling Lane" indicating that the mound could be the site of a meeting place.

Dode church consists of a nave, chancel of coarsed flints and a south doorway. Although no longer used for regular worship for more than 350 years, the church is used for weddings and private prayer. Dode church is open to the public on Sunday afternoons from Easter until October. The floor is strewn with straw and autumn herb-scented leaves. It is only lit by candles.

Dover St James

The town and port of Dover had seven churches in Medieval times, which were St James, St John, St Martin le Grand, St Mary in Castro (in the castle), St Mary the Virgin, St Nicholas and St Peter. Only those of St Mary in Castro and St Mary the Virgin are in use today. The others are now lost. There is also a chapel, dedicated to St Edmund in Dover, which was built by St Richard of Chichester in 1253. It is still in use today.

Of the lost churches only that of St James has any visible remains above ground. It was a Saxon building and is thought to be one of the three churches mentioned in the Domesday Book of 1086 for Dover. The present church dates from the early 12th century and consisted of a central tower, nave, chancel, south and north aisles. At the west end of the nave is a doorway.

The church was also used as a meeting place for the official courts of the Barons of the Cinque Ports as well as a place of worship. It was restored and enlarged in the 19th century and there were 17th and 18th century monuments inside it. The building was badly damaged by a bomb during World War II in February 1945. The church now stands in ruins and is open to the public to view. The central tower has gone but the west doorway still exists.

Eastbridge

The ruins of Eastbridge church, about two miles east of Newchurch on the Romney Marsh, stand in overgrowth. It originally consisted of a tower, nave and chancel of the 14th century built on the site of a Saxon church. It was made with quarry stone and has been in ruins since the 15th century after the village, which it served, was lost during the plague.

The only remains of the church today are fragments of the tower and the west wall of the nave. The site was excavated in 1913 and revealed the plan of the chancel, which was irregular. Eastbridge is mentioned in the Domesday Book and two churches are recorded. The second church was that at Dymchurch, some three miles to the south.

Eastwell

The ancient church at Eastwell near Ashford, dedicated to St Mary, was destroyed by a bomb in World War II. It originally consisted of a square battlemented tower, nave, two chancels, north and south aisles. It is built of flint with ashlar stone round the windows. There is a tomb in the church, which is said to be that of Richard III's son "Richard Plantagenet" who is reputed to have come to Eastwell after escaping from the Battle of Bosworth.

All that remains of the church today is the tower, parts of the nave and vestry. Before the damage there was an ancient flint-knapped cross on the eastern wall. Although in ruins the church remains consecrated and the churchyard is sacred ground. The ruins of the church are adjacent to a large lake. The park around the church was where the original village of Eastwell once existed.

Ebony

The village and church of Ebony, some two miles east of Appledore, originally stood on a hill on the Isle of Oxney. The church, dedicated to St Mary, consisted of a nave, chancel and bell turret. It was a much larger building in Medieval times and during a storm in Elizabethan times was struck by lightning and burnt down, leaving it in ruins. A smaller church or chapel was later built on the foundations.

In 1858 the church was demolished because it was in an inaccessible position and in a bad state of repair. In the same year a new church was built at Ebony, also dedicated to St Mary, further to the north at Reading Street. Stones from the old church were used in its construction. On the site of the original church on the hill called "Chapel Bank" is the graveyard which was still used for burials until fairly recently.

Fawkenhurst

Fawkenhurst, overlooking the Romney Marsh, was in ancient times called "Falconers Hurst" from a family. Today it is sometimes marked as Hurst or Falconhurst on O/S maps. The church dedicated to St Leonard was in ruins from 1530 and today no sign of it exists above ground. Its site is marked by a cross on a stepped plinth and is on private farmland.

Although a lost church, with only its site remaining with the cross marking it, services were still held there once a year in June until the 1980s. An altar was made up of two bales of straw and wooden benches were provided for the congregation. This would have been a perfect setting for an annual evensong on a summer evening.

Hope All Saints

The ruins of Hope All Saints church to the north-west of New Romney stand on a mound in a field where no road leads to it. The only other buildings nearby are those of Chapel Farm. The church consisted of a Norman nave and chancel and has been in ruins since the middle of the 17th century. By the late 19th century the walls were almost complete, but it was roofless.

There was a chancel arch, five windows on the nave and a carved door of the 12th century. Today the ruins consist of six chunks of masonry and the north-eastern one is smaller than it was in the late 1970s. It is visible from the nearby road and there is a style and footpath across the field to the south of it. The Medieval bell from Hope All Saints is now in St Nicholas church at New Romney.

Horne's Place Chapel

Horne's Place at Appledore Heath is a Medieval timber-framed house. The chapel next to it was built in 1366 by William Horne. It is short, but high, being 22 feet in length and 23 feet in height. It was a private chapel attached to the manor of Horne's Place. The chapel has a large Perpendicular east window and a north and south window with carved tracery. Its rood is panelled with moulded arches on stone corbals. There is evidence that a pre-existing building had been modified to create the chapel. It is owned by English Heritage and is only open by appointment.

Horton

The Medieval chapel at Horton near Chartham dates from either the late 13th or early 14th century. It consisted of a nave with buttresses, chancel and a late 14th century bell turret. On the north wall was a single light trefoil-headed window and a west window on the nave. It was built with Caen stone, flint and Kentish Ragstone. In the chapel is a chancel arch with mouldings and a piscina.

The chapel probably closed for worship at the Dissolution in the 16th century and was in use as a granary in the 19th century. Today the chapel stands in overgrowth by Horton Farm. All walls are still complete, but it is roofless. A few decorative details exist inside today apart from the mouldings, chancel arch and piscina. The chapel walls are held up by boards and scaffolding for support.

Little Chart

Little Chart church, dedicated to St Mary, was built in three stages between 1200 and 1500. It consisted of a tower, nave and chancel. The church was damaged by a German VI Doodlebug flying bomb on August 16 1944. No one was killed, but it severely ruined the church. A new church was built at Little Chart in 1955 and during its construction services were occasionally held in the ruins of the old church.

The ruins of the old church consist of most of the tower, the north and south walls of the nave and some tiles are still in situ on the floor. The church was in too bad a state of repair, but the ruins were made safe and are accessible for the public to view. Monuments from the old church were saved and are now in the new church, one of which is of the Darell family.

Maidstone St Faith

Maidstone was mentioned in the Domesday Book as "Meddestone", where a church was recorded. This small Saxon building was originally dedicated to St Mary and in 1395 it was rebuilt as a collegiate church dedicated to All Saints. Other chapels existed in Maidstone in Medieval times dedicated to St Faith, St John, St Peter and St Anne.

That of St Anne was an allusion made by Hasted in the folio edition of his history and it was omitted in his octave edition. There are certain lands referred to called Perryfield and Caring "beside the chapel of St Anne", but as no other reference has been found, then Hasted may have made a mistake. The chapel of St John, which was in existence in the mid-15th century, stood on the east side of Lower Stone Street where a piece of land "Chapel Croft" existed. St John's chapel was mentioned in the 16th century and was probably out of use by then. No sign of it exists today.

St Faith's church or free chapel was built in the 13th century and closed for worship in 1634, but was reopened in 1646 for nonconformists for 90 years. In the 18th century it was used as a public hall and then a girls' boarding school. It was finally pulled down in 1858 and on the site today is the modern church of St Faith, which was built in 1871. The only remains of the original St Faith's are pillars with capitals and bases erected in the museum garden nearby.

Maidstone St Peter

The church dedicated to St Peter was built as a chapel in the 13th century to the hospital called "Le Newerk de Maydestones". The hospital itself was dedicated to St Peter and St Paul and built to shelter Pilgrims to give them rest on their long journey from Winchester to Canterbury. The hospital continued until 1395 and at the Dissolution was sold to Lord Cobham. The chapel fell into disuse and was in use as a store room at the beginning of the 19th century.

In 1836 the chapel was enlarged and became a parish church dedicated to St Peter and services commenced in 1837. The church consists of a nave, chancel, north and south transepts. The transepts were added when it became a parish church. In the church is a figure of St Peter holding keys to Heaven's gate and a cockerel crowing at his feet. There is also a piscina and sedilla in the church. St Peter's church closed for worship in 1982 and is now in use as a nursery.

Maplescombe

The ruined church at Maplescombe, some two miles north of West Kingsdown, stands in a field by a farm. It is early Norman in date and consisted of a nave and apsidal chancel and has been in ruins for centuries. It probably came out of use soon after the village which stood around it was lost at the time of the Black Death. The walls of the church are of a great thickness and the windows had some circular arches.

On the site today the west wall of the nave still stands and only fragments of the north and south walls remain. The ruins are very overgrown with elder trees, nettles and ivy. Human bones have turned up occasionally by ploughing nearby mainly on the south side of the church. This was the graveyard. The village, but not its church, was mentioned in the Domesday Book as Mapledescam.

Midley

The church at Midley two miles or so south of Old Romney, has been in ruins since the 16th century. It was probably a small church of the 15th century built on the site of a Saxon one which was mentioned in the Domesday Book. Only the west wall of the church remains today, standing by itself in a field, which can be seen from a distance. It was built mainly of pale yellowish bricks and there are traces of a door and window on the west wall. The arch over the former is Gothic. Midley was the middle island between Lydd and Old Romney where a village once existed.

Newlands Chapel

The chapel at Newlands Studd, some two miles south-west of Charing, was built in the late Norman period with rubble stone and some Caen stone dressings. It consisted of a nave, chancel and south aisle. The latter no longer exists. It has a north doorway and two pilaster buttresses in the south wall. There are carvings on the south side. The chapel is situated in the grounds of a Medieval timber-framed house. It came out of use a few centuries ago and is now in use as a store room.

New Romney St Martin

The Cinque port town of New Romney had a total of five churches in Medieval times, which were St John, St Lawrence, St Martin, St Michael, and St Nicholas. Only the Norman church of St Nicholas is still standing and in regular use today, and all the others are lost probably due to New Romney declining in size during the Middle Ages. There are no visible remains of these churches today.

The parish church of St Martin dates from the Saxon period and was the oldest church in New Romney. It was built on the site of an Anglo-Saxon oratory of St Martin, which dates from the 8th century. The church consisted of a tower, nave, chancel and aisles. It became an appendant chapel to St Nicholas in the Medieval period.

In the early part of the 16th century the chancel was in danger of falling down from decay, and was not repaired. The church was demolished in the mid-16th century after Archbishop Cranmer authorised its destruction, and materials from it were sold to help the poor. On the site today is a large open space called "St Martin's Field".

Old Soar

The old chapel at Old Soar near Plaxtol was a manorial chapel to a manor house of 1290. It was built as a private chapel for the Culpeper family and was also used as an office. Today an 18th century red brick house stands on the site of the hall. The solar chamber next to it stands on a barrel-vaulted undercroft and the square block at the back is a garderobe or latrine block. This is where clothing was often stored.

The chapel itself is rectangular and projects from the solar chamber from the east end. It has a large east window and on the south wall is a piscina, which was used for washing vessels for prayer. By the east window is a carved corbel, which served as a stand for an image or candle. The site is owned by the National Trust and is open from April to September. There is an exhibition room beneath the chapel.

Orgarswick

The ancient church of Orgarswick on the Romney Marsh near Dymchurch was probably built in the 11th or 12th century and was a single-chambered building. The village which it served was deserted in the Middle Ages due to the plague and the church fell into ruin sometime in the 16th or 17th centuries. All that remains of the church today are its foundations and a few stones marked by a cross and a plaque near Chapel Farm. The cross itself is made up of stones from the old church.

Oxney

Situated in a wood east of the A258 Dover to Deal road stands the ruins of Oxney church, which is dedicated to St Nicholas. It was once a parish church of the early 12th century and probably fell into ruin in the 16th century. The church consisted of a Norman nave, chancel and a south aisle. The village was probably deserted during the Black Death of the mid-14th century.

The walls of the church still remain standing today and in the north wall of the chancel are original windows. There is a similar window in the north wall of the nave and also a 14th century window. The most interesting feature of the ruined church is the blocked arcade of the 13th century on the south wall. This would have been blocked when the south aisle came out of use.

Paddlesworth

Paddlesworth, about a mile west of Snodland, was mentioned in the Domesday Book as "Pellesorde" and a church was recorded. The village was deserted by the Black Death in the mid-14th century, leaving a few houses and an ancient church. The church is on the Pilgrims Way and the Pilgrims would have used it for centuries. The building was closed for worship in 1678 after people no longer lived in the village. It was at one time used as a barn.

Paddlesworth church, dedicated to St Benedict, is a Norman building on the site of a Saxon one. It consists of a nave, chancel, north door and 13th century chancel arch. There are no original windows surviving on the walls today. There is a blocked door on the north wall of the chancel. The church is open to the public at weekends and is well worth a visit.

Reculver

The parish church at Reculver with its twin towers dedicated to St Mary was built within the walls of the Roman fort of Regulbium. A church has existed on the site since the 7th century AD and had a nave some 37 feet long and an apsidal chancel. The church was enlarged in the 8th century and was further enlarged in the 12th century when the twin towers which had spires, were built.

Due to encroachments of the sea, the church was abandoned at the beginning of the 19th century and a new church was built further inland at Hillborough, using materials from the old one. The ruins of the church, which consist of the twin towers, walls at the east end and other remains, are a distinctive feature on the north coast of Kent. It and the fort are owned by English Heritage. They are open all year round.

Rochester Bridge Chapel

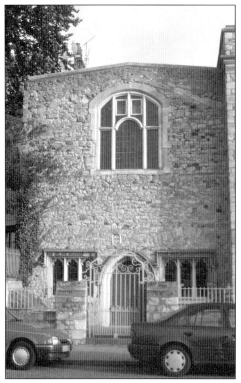

The city of Rochester was built within the walls of the Roman town and has a cathedral, two churches and a castle. Only one of the churches "St Margaret's" is in use today and the other "St Nicholas" is in use for another function. Also there was a bridge chapel and leper hospital chapel. The present cathedral stands on the site of a Saxon one and the line of its apsidal chancel is marked out inside the western end of the cathedral. The west end of the Saxon cathedral stood outside where there is a plaque.

The bridge chapel, which stood at the east end of the stone bridge was built in the 14th century. It was constructed of ragstone and used by travellers passing through Rochester. The stone bridge was 570 feet in length and had eleven arches. This bridge was demolished in the 19th century and a new one was constructed some 40 yards to the north. The latter is on the site of the Roman bridge, which carried Watling Street across the Medway.

The bridge chapel fell into ruin after the Dissolution of the Monasteries, but it was let for other purposes now and again. It was in use as a fruit and sweet shop in the middle of the Victorian period. The bridge chapel was restored in 1937 and was re-windowed. It is open to the public a few times each year.

Rochester St Bartholomew's Chapel

The chapel dedicated to St Bartholomew is situated at the far eastern end of Rochester in the High Street. It was built in 1124 by Hugh de Trottiscliffe (a monk in Rochester) as part of the leper hospital. The latter was founded by Bishop Gundolph in 1078 and was moved to a new site in New Road in 1863.

The chapel itself fell into disuse sometime in the 16th century and was restored in 1896 by Gilbert Scott. It was used for residential purposes; at present it is not occupied and is up for sale. The chapel consists of a nave, chancel, apsidal chantry, a short spire, north aisle and vestry. The latter two were added by Scott at his restoration. There is a pillar and piscina in the vestry.

Rochester St Nicholas

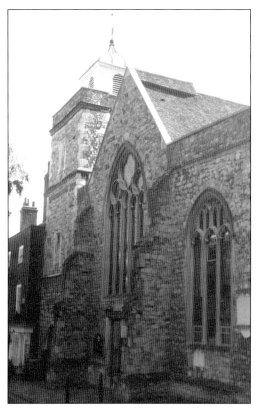

The church dedicated to St Nicholas was built in the 15th century as the parish church of the city in the cathedral churchyard. Before it was built parishioners used the cathedral nave for worship. The church consists of a north-west tower, nave, chancel and south aisle. The building was in a bad state of repair in 1621 and was restored in 1624.

There are several 17th century monuments in the church such as that of Thomas Rocke 1635, which is a small tablet with kneeling figures. There is a Perpendicular concave-sided font, cup and paten covers of 1602 and 1609. The church closed for worship in 1964 and became the administration offices for the Diocese of Rochester as it is today.

Ruxley

The ancient church of Rokesle (now Ruxley) has been in ruins for centuries. In 1557 a note from Sir Martin Bowes reads, "that the parish church of Rokesle, the profits of which did not exceed the sum of six pounds was much decayed and ruinous, as well in the steeple, as in the walls and roof". The note also includes "praying therefore, that the church might be suppressed and wholly demolished".

Ruxley church was not wholly demolished for the chancel still remains today. It was in use as a barn and there were plans to make the church into a restaurant. It stands in the grounds of a garden centre and the area just north of the building was landscaped to create a Medieval garden.

Saint Blaise Chapel

The history of St Blaise chapel at Blaise Farm south of Offham is unusual. It dates from either the 11th or 12th century and was given to the Hospital of St Mary, Strood by Richard I in c.1190. This hospital's income included the chapel in 1534, which was worth £2 then. It was also mentioned in wills of 1475 and 1557. It probably became disused and left to go to ruin in the 16th century.

The chapel, according to C H Fielding in the early part of the 20th century, "would appear to have been a small church with nave and apse". It consisted of two buildings, which formed an L-shape plan. One building faced north to south and the other east to west. On the site today are foundations and bits of masonry covered by a small woodland in a field east of a footpath.

Saint Paul's Cray

The parish church of St Paul's Cray, dedicated to St Paulinus, dates from the early 13th century and was built in flintstone. It stands on the site of an earlier church which was mentioned in the Domesday Book and possibly goes back to Anglo-Saxon times. It consists of a tower, spire, nave, chancel, north-east chapel and south aisle. There was once a north aisle and arcading can still be seen on the north wall of the nave.

Roman tiles are visible on the walls of the church and when an air-raid shelter was being built in the Second World War a Roman brick kiln was found. In the church is a cup of 1718 and several monuments. One of these is a 13th century coffin lid with a cross on it. The church became redundant in 1978 and is now in use as office accommodation.

Sandling

The chapel dedicated to St Andrew at Sandling, two miles north of Maidstone, was probably built in the 15th century for pilgrims to hear mass before they proceeded to the abbey at nearby Boxley. It was part of the Boxley Abbey Estate and contained a holy relic said to be the little finger of St Andrew, which was encased in silver. A local legend has it that a tunnel connects the chapel to the abbey.

The chapel probably came out of use after the Dissolution and was incorporated into another building. There was probably accommodation for a priest. It is a small sandstone building with Perpendicular windows on the south side, which was described as "a pair of cottages" in 1870. It was in part a shop and also a post office for Sandling, but at present it is not occupied at all.

Sandwich St Mary

There were three parish churches in Sandwich in Medieval times and were St Clement, St Mary and St Peter. Only that of St Clement is in use today and the others are redundant. The church dedicated to St Mary's stands on the oldest Christian site in Sandwich. A convent was founded here in the 7th century AD. The convent was destroyed by the Danes and rebuilt by King Canute's wife "Emma". The church was built at the beginning of the 12th century and was set fire by the French in the 14th century.

The church was restored in the 15th century. It had a central tower, spire, nave, chancel, south and north aisles and two chapels. It was damaged by an earthquake in 1578 and when the tower collapsed in 1668 it brought down most of the remaining church. The building was restored shortly afterwards and services resumed in 1675.

The church was closed for worship in 1948 and the roof was damaged by a severe gale in 1954. In 1956 a request was made to demolish the church, but the Friends of St Mary's Sandwich was formed to keep it, and money was raised and the church was saved. It is open to the public and there are monuments, a 15th century font and other items of interest to see.

Sandwich St Peter

The church dedicated to St Peter in Sandwich dates from the 13th century on the site of a Norman building, which was probably destroyed by French raids in 1216. Part of the Norman church can be seen at the west end of the nave. It consists of a nave, chancel, central tower, south and north aisles and also a north porch.

The upper parts of the central tower collapsed in 1661, which destroyed the south aisle in the process. The church was rebuilt in the 17th century (apart from the south aisle) and was in use as a place of worship until 1948. It is now redundant and contains monuments, a fire pump and remains of wall paintings. It is open to the public and is well worth a visit.

In the churchyard to the west of the nave is some masonry, which has a 14th century window. This came from the chapel of St Thomas Hospital and was re-erected in the church grounds in 1923. The St Thomas Hospital was founded in Sandwich by Thomas Ellys in 1392. Thomas Ellys' tomb is inside St Peter's church.

Seasalter

Seasalter, to the west of Whitstable, was mentioned in the Domesday Book and a church was recorded. This Saxon church was built in the 11th century. The Archbishop of Canterbury "Alphege" was murdered in 1011 at Greenwich and was buried in St Paul's. His remains were taken to Canterbury to be interred in the cathedral in 1023 and on the way his bones were housed in Seasalter church for three days.

The church was originally dedicated to St Peter and then became St Alphege in the archbishop's honour. This Saxon church ended up being lost to sea by coastal erosion way back in 1090. The foundations of the church were uncovered during a storm in 1799. Today nothing can be seen of the church at low tide, although some stones seem to look like the foundations of a building. Could this be the site of the church?

A new church dedicated to St Alphege was built further inland at Seasalter in the 12th century. A nave was built in 1616, but was demolished in 1845. The chancel became a burial chapel and all services were resumed. Another church dedicated to St Alphege was also built in Whitstable High Street in 1845 and several things from the old church are in it.

Snave

The parish church of Snave on the Romney Marsh, dedicated to St Augustine, dates from the 13th century, and was probably built on the site of a small Saxon church. It consists of a battlemented tower, nave, chancel, north chapel and south porch. The north chapel became a schoolroom, where a fireplace was fitted, and then the church vestry. The church is heavily buttressed.

In the church are the remains of a bowl of a 13th century font, a piscina in both the chancel and chapel, and three bells in the tower. One of the bells is one of only three surviving from the foundry of Stephen Norton of Maidstone c.1380. In the north wall of the nave is a carved stone with skull and crossbones. There are some monuments on the walls.

Due to a small population at Snave the church became redundant in 1983 and is now maintained by the Romney Marsh Historic Churches Trust. Only one service is held each year, which is "Harvest" on the second Sunday in September. The church is known as "The Daffodil Church" because there is an avenue of daffodils leading up to it and a great number in the churchyard. It is well worth a visit in the springtime.

Stone Chapel

The ruins of Stone chapel west of Faversham are situated in a field north of the A2 main road, which runs along the Roman road "Watling Street". It stands on the site of a mid-4th century Roman temple part of which was incorporated in the chancel of the later church. This is the only known example in Britain of a Roman temple being used in a Christian church, and it is still visible as part of the chancel, where there is ragstone and Roman brick.

The chapel was possibly built in the 7th century AD, using the old Roman temple, and an apse was added in the 11th century. Both nave and chancel were extended in the 13th century and the building was dedicated to Our Lady of Elwarton. The chapel was abandoned sometime in the 16th century; foundations and walls remain visible today and there is a plaque on the site. It is owned by English Heritage and open all year round.

Swingfield

The chapel of St John at Swingfield was built in the early 13th century. It was the chapel which formed part of the Commanding of the Knights Hospitallers. It consists of a two-storey hall with a north-west porch. It underwent alterations in the past and the western part was converted in the early 16th century for residential purposes. The foundations for the choir stalls and screen were found during excavations in 1977.

Upper Halling

In the parish of Halling, some three-quarters of a mile west of the village church, is Upper Halling with an old free chapel dedicated to St Lawrence. It is either late 12th or early 13th century in date, and was used for Pilgrims who travelled from Canterbury to Winchester in Medieval times. The chapel was suppressed by an act in 1547 and was in use as a workshop in the 18th century.

The chapel is tallish and situated at the junctions of Chapel Lane and The Street. In the 19th century it was converted into cottages called "Chapel Houses". The chapel is at the eastern end of the cottages and has angled buttresses at its east end, a head of a lancet window on the south wall and a large thin window on the east wall. The building still contains a font.

Warden

The church at Warden, dedicated to St James on the Isle of Sheppey some two miles east of Eastchurch, dates from the Medieval period. It consisted of a nave, chancel and bell turret. In 1836 a tower was added using stones from the old London Bridge, which was demolished in 1832. At this time the village which it served only had a few houses.

The church stood near the edge of a treacherous cliff at Warden Point in the 19th century. Due to threats of cliff erosion (a farmhouse and outbuildings having been carried away due to a landslip in 1809), the church became in a bad state of repair and was demolished in 1887. Shortly after this the site of the church ended up succumbing to the sea. Nothing of the church or village can be seen at low tide.

Well

The chapel at Well in the parish of Ickham probably dates from the 14th century when Robert de Solbury was instituted Rector of Ickham, cum capella de Welle, in 1351. It consisted of a bell tower, nave and chancel and had the facilities of a parish church. It had a west door with a window above, east window, south door, possibly a north door and a holy water stoup. There was also a graveyard.

The chapel's dedication is unknown, but it is suggested that it was to St Thomas because Richard Grant of Ickham bequested in 1514 "The chapel of St Thomas in the same parish". This must have referred to Well chapel. In the 16th century the chapel came out of use and fell into ruin. Today parts of all four walls remain standing in a field by a path. Well is named from the spring water which forms the Little Stour river only a few yards away.

West Hythe

The church at West Hythe dedicated to the Blessed Virgin Mary was a small Norman building which consisted of a nave and chancel and was built of course stone. It has been in ruins for several centuries, probably from the early part of the 16th century. This may have been due to the village having been deserted by the Black Death in the 14th century.

On the site today four walls of the nave are still standing, including the pointed archway between the nave and chancel. The latter is Gothic as is the west door. Re-used Roman brick was used over the west door and also in a small window on the south wall of the nave. There is also a blocked south doorway. No sign of the chancel exists above ground today.